GW01326478

Original title:
Healthy Transformation

Author: Tim Wood

ISBN HARDBACK: 978-9916-88-322-8
ISBN PAPERBACK: 978-9916-88-323-5

Mosaic of Moments

In twilight's glow we stand still,
Collecting fragments, heart's thrill.
Each laugh, each tear, a piece we keep,
In memory's quilt, our treasures sleep.

Across the years, paths intertwine,
Colors blend, hearts align.
Moments dance, both fierce and mild,
In this canvas, we're forever styled.

The Horizon Within

Beyond the skies, a dreamer roams,
Chasing visions, finding homes.
In the heart's depth, adventures call,
A world inside, where spirits thrall.

With every dawn, we rise anew,
The horizon gleams with shades of blue.
Through trials past, our strength is born,
Inward journeys, rebirth is sworn.

Whispers of Renewal

In the quiet woods, secrets stir,
Nature's whispers gently blur.
Each leaf awakens, kissed by light,
A promise blooms, dispelling night.

With every breath, old shadows fade,
In growth's embrace, we're unafraid.
Seasons change, yet we remain,
In the cycle, joy and pain.

Blossoms of Change

In gardens bright, new colors shine,
Each petal tells of tales divine.
Through storms we weather, roots run deep,
In the soil of hope, our dreams we keep.

As summer fades, the autumn rolls,
Transformation sings within our souls.
With every fall, new life begins,
In nature's dance, the heart still wins.

Beyond the Horizon's Edge

In twilight's glow, the colors blend,
Whispers of dreams, where shadows bend.
The sea calls out, its secrets deep,
Across the waves, the visions sweep.

Stars ignite as night descends,
Journey unknown, yet hope transcends.
Beneath the sky, horizons wide,
Hearts unchained, we sail the tide.

Mountains rise and rivers flow,
Through trials faced, our spirits grow.
With every step, a path laid bare,
To seek the light, we must dare.

Beyond the edge, where lost souls meet,
In unity, our fears retreat.
Together strong, we forge ahead,
Beyond the horizon, where dreams are fed.

Leaves of Transformation

In autumn's breeze, the leaves conspire,
To shed their gold, ignite the fire.
Each fluttering drift, a tale to tell,
Of time's embrace, where shadows dwell.

Branches bare, yet filled with grace,
Embrace the change, the slow-paced race.
In rust and red, a new allure,
From what has been, we will endure.

With every fall, new roots will grow,
A cycle rich, the earth will show.
In whispered winds, the stories weave,
Of metamorphosis, we believe.

From ashes rise, a phoenix song,
In unity, we all belong.
As leaves descend, we find our way,
In transformation, we seize the day.

Whispers of Wellness

In quiet corners, peace will bloom,
Soft whispers chase away the gloom.
With gentle waves, the heart's embrace,
Wellness finds its rightful place.

Breathe in life, let worries part,
Each moment calming, a soothing art.
Nature's song, a tender call,
In whispers, we can stand tall.

The Symphony of Change

Notes of life in motion play,
Change composes night and day.
Each transition, a graceful dance,
In every shift, we find our chance.

Echoes hum, a new refrain,
In struggle, there is never pain.
Embrace the flow, let go of fears,
The symphony grows through the years.

Blossoming Spirit

Seeds of hope in hearts reside,
With nurturing hands, we confide.
From shadows deep, joy will rise,
A blossoming spirit greets the skies.

Colors vibrant, each petal shines,
In the warmth of love, the spirit aligns.
Courage springs forth, breaking free,
As flowers unveil their destiny.

A Tapestry of Growth

Threads of experience woven tight,
In every stitch, there's wisdom's light.
Patterns form through joy and strife,
A tapestry tells the tale of life.

Fingers dance, creating new,
With every choice, a journey true.
Embracing change, we find our worth,
In this grand fabric, we find our earth.

Navigating New Waters

A boat drifts on the tide,
Charting courses wide and far,
Stars above, a guiding light,
Waves whispering of dreams to spar.

New horizons call my name,
Courage found in every swell,
With the winds, I play the game,
In the sea, my hopes compel.

Through storms and calms, I roam,
Finding treasures in the blue,
Each ripple feels like home,
In the heart, the ocean's hue.

Navigating worlds unseen,
With every wave, I start anew,
In this journey, I am keen,
To find the depths that feel like true.

The Blooming Path

Along a trail where flowers grow,
Petals dance in morning's light,
Colors burst, a vibrant show,
Nature's beauty, pure delight.

With each step, the fragrance sweet,
Whispers of the earth arise,
In the sun, the blossoms greet,
Opening their arms to skies.

Through the shadows, blooms appear,
Hope is woven in each stem,
Every bud, a sign we steer,
Towards the joy that we condemn.

Walking softly, heart in hand,
In this garden, trust shall sway,
Life unfolds, a blooming land,
On this path, I'll find my way.

Awakening the Self

In the silence, echoes breathe,
Awakening a sleeping soul,
Finding strength in every wreath,
Whispers beckon, make me whole.

Mirror reflects the truth within,
Layers shed, like autumn leaves,
In the stillness, I begin,
To unravel what one believes.

With the dawn, new light descends,
Illuminating hidden fears,
Every heartbeat transcends,
Washing away forgotten tears.

Embracing change, I stand tall,
Finding solace in the now,
In this journey, I'll not fall,
Awakening, I take a bow.

Waves of Transformation

Cresting tides pull me along,
Change crashes like the ocean's roar,
In each swell, I find my song,
Transforming what I was before.

The surf ignites a spark so bright,
Cleansing shadows in its wake,
In this dance of day and night,
New beginnings softly break.

As I ride this ebb and flow,
Lessons learned in every tide,
Through the chaos, I shall grow,
In the waves, my fears subside.

Rising up, I find my grace,
Emerging strong, I face the rise,
Waves of change, a warm embrace,
In the depths, my spirit flies.

The Light Beyond the Rain

The storm may darken skies,
Yet hope begins to rise.
Through puddles, colors gleam,
A brighter world, a dream.

Raindrops kiss the earth,
Awakening new birth.
In every drop, a light,
Guides us through the night.

The clouds begin to part,
A glow ignites the heart.
In whispers, nature sings,
Of joy that laughter brings.

So let us dance in rain,
With hearts free from the pain.
For every tear we shed,
Brings light where we have tread.

Radiant Paths to Tomorrow

Each dawn brings a new chance,
To weave life's vibrant dance.
With hope like morning light,
We step towards the bright.

Paths may twist and turn,
Yet in struggle, we learn.
Through shadows, courage flows,
As the future glows.

With hearts aligned and bold,
We chase dreams yet untold.
Together, hand in hand,
We journey through this land.

Radiant dreams take flight,
As stars adorn the night.
With every step we take,
New worlds begin to wake.

Echoes of the Future

In quiet moments shared,
Whispers of dreams declared.
The past may fade away,
But echoes here will stay.

In the stillness, we find,
The stories left behind.
Their lessons gently call,
To rise and never fall.

Through time's vast, flowing stream,
We build upon a dream.
With every choice we make,
New paths, new hearts awake.

Listen close, hear the sound,
Of hopes that gather round.
The future sings with grace,
In every heart, a place.

Shifting Perspectives

When clouds obscure the view,
Look deeper for what's true.
A shift can clear the haze,
Revealing brighter days.

Through another's eyes we see,
The world in harmony.
Each story holds a key,
To set the spirit free.

In difference, strength we find,
Connections growing blind.
Embrace the shapes we take,
For understanding's sake.

Let colors blend and meld,
In unity, we're held.
Different views ignite change,
Transform the world we arrange.

The Journey Within

In silence I tread, a path unknown,
Whispers of dreams in the depth they've grown.
Amid the shadows, light starts to weave,
Finding the strength I never believed.

With each step taken, the heart beats clear,
Unraveling secrets, confronting the fear.
The map is my soul, with scars that guide,
Embracing the truth that I cannot hide.

Embracing New Horizons

Beyond the mountains, a horizon gleams,
Each sunrise whispers, igniting new dreams.
Winds of change beckon, wings spread wide,
Adventure awaits, and I cannot hide.

Clouds of doubt drift, as bright skies appear,
With hope in my heart, I conquer my fear.
Steps toward the future I willingly take,
As the dawn breaks, new paths I will make.

Metamorphosis of the Soul

In cocooned silence, the spirit transforms,
Breaking the shell where vulnerability norms.
Emerging like spring, vibrant and free,
Embracing the changes, becoming me.

With colors of courage, I paint my flight,
Through trials endured, I'll shine ever bright.
The journey is sacred, each tear and smile,
Every step forward is worth every trial.

Risen from the Ashes

From fiery depths, I ascend anew,
With lessons in heart, strength born from rue.
Like a phoenix bold, I spread my wings,
In the warmth of rebirth, my spirit sings.

Resilience carved deep, I stand with grace,
Echoes of trials no longer disgrace.
The ashes of sorrow are now my crown,
In the light of my story, I wear no frown.

Reflections in Bloom

In the garden where dreams reside,
Petals whisper secrets, wide.
Colors dance in the soft light,
Every moment feels just right.

Mirrors of the heart unfold,
Tales of love that never grow old.
Each hue a story to be told,
In the warmth where souls are bold.

Journey Toward Wholeness

Steps upon the winding trail,
With every breath, I shall not fail.
Lessons learned, both great and small,
In the silence, I hear the call.

Mountains high and valleys deep,
Awakening from restless sleep.
With every stride, I find my place,
A journey wrapped in time and grace.

Renewal's Gentle Touch

A breeze whispers through the trees,
Life returns with subtle ease.
Nature's brush strokes on the dawn,
Awakening dreams as night is drawn.

In the heart, a spark ignites,
Filling shadows with the lights.
Every breath a chance to mend,
In the warmth of spring, we blend.

The Path of the Lotus

From muddy depths, a bloom ascends,
With grace and strength, it never bends.
Each petal holds a tale of strife,
Rising up to share its life.

Sunlight dances on the lake,
In stillness, ripples softly wake.
The lotus teaches how to soar,
Embracing all that came before.

The Rising Sun

Golden rays break through the night,
Softly warming the morning light.
Whispers dance on the gentle breeze,
A promise of hope among the trees.

Colors blend in a glorious hue,
The world awakens, fresh and new.
Birds sing joyfully on the wing,
Nature rejoices, beginning to sing.

Shadows fade as brightness grows,
In every heart, a thrill that flows.
The dawn ignites a brand new way,
Embrace the magic of the day.

Rays of gold brush the barren land,
Life emerges at the sun's command.
With every moment that we gain,
Hope springs forth through joy and pain.

Chase the Chill Away

When winter's grip holds all in sway,
Kindle warmth, chase the chill away.
Gather friends 'round the fire's glow,
Share the light as the cold winds blow.

Frosty breath in the quiet air,
Laughter rings, dispelling despair.
Hot cocoa sips and stories told,
Hearts grow warmer, against the cold.

Beneath the stars, our spirits rise,
The moon is bright in velvet skies.
Hold on tight, as seasons sway,
Together we'll chase the chill away.

For every shadow, there's a light,
Courage gathers through darkest night.
With love and laughter, we find our way,
In unity, we chase the chill away.

Unfolding Petals of Purpose

In the garden where dreams take flight,
Petals open, revealing delight.
Each hue tells a tale so sweet,
Life awakens at our feet.

Every blossom a wish unspun,
Beneath the warmth of the gentle sun.
With every layer, we find our path,
Embracing joy, facing the wrath.

As branches sway in the soft spring air,
Hope unfolds with beauty rare.
To nurture dreams, we plant our seeds,
In every heart, a garden of needs.

Watch us bloom through trials and tears,
In unity, we conquer fears.
The fragrance whispers, a soft embrace,
Unfolding petals, our sacred space.

Bonds of the Present

Moments woven, a vibrant thread,
In this life, where we are led.
With every heartbeat, we find our way,
Together we shape our every day.

Laughter echoes in the shared light,
Through trials faced, we hold on tight.
Time may wander, yet here we stand,
In bonds of the present, hand in hand.

Memories linger, sweet and bright,
Illuminated by love's soft light.
In every smile and soft embrace,
We find our strength, our sacred place.

Though the clock ticks, we shall remain,
Informed by joy, not marked by pain.
With every moment that we invest,
We forge the future, we've been blessed.

Threads of Possibility

In whispers of the dawn,
Dreams weave through the air.
Each choice a stepping stone,
New paths begin to flare.

The tapestry unfolds,
With colors bright and bold.
A dance of fate we hold,
As futures then behold.

With courage, hearts align,
We venture into light.
The threads of hope combine,
To weave a world so bright.

In shadows, visions gleam,
Potential starts to soar.
Within this waking dream,
We find forevermore.

Unveiling the Radiant Self

Beneath the layers worn,
A spark awaits to shine.
In silence, truth is born,
To leave the dark behind.

In mirror's gaze, we seek,
Reflections pure and clear.
Our voices strong, unique,
In harmony we steer.

The masks begin to fade,
As essence takes its place.
With courage, unafraid,
We dare embrace our grace.

In every heartbeats' song,
The rhythm of our souls.
Together we belong,
As one, we make it whole.

Nature's Embrace

In whispers of the trees,
The breeze sings soft and low.
Each petal, every leaf,
In symphony they flow.

The mountains rise so grand,
With valleys tucked below.
In nature's gentle hand,
We find our peace and glow.

With rivers tracing trails,
And skies, a canvas pure.
The heartbeat of the world,
In soft embrace, endure.

Each sunset paints the night,
With dreams that intertwine.
In nature's warm delight,
Our spirits, free, will shine.

Renewal's Melody

In spring's embrace we bloom,
New life begins to stir.
With every vibrant hue,
The earth begins to purr.

The cycle spins anew,
With raindrops soft and sweet.
Each moment brings a chance,
To rise upon our feet.

As seasons shift and sway,
We gather strength to mend.
In every dawn's replay,
Our hearts begin to blend.

With joy, we sing aloud,
In harmony we find.
Renewal's sweet refrain,
Awakens heart and mind.

Transcendent Steps

In quiet moments, we ascend,
Each footfall whispers, we transcend.
The path unfolds, a sacred line,
Where shadows fade and spirits shine.

With every breath, we touch the sky,
Our hearts ablaze, we learn to fly.
The world, a canvas, wide and bright,
Each step we take ignites the light.

Through valleys deep and mountains high,
We journey forth, we will not die.
For in the dance of life's embrace,
We find our strength, we find our place.

So let us walk with grace and trust,
In every step, in every gust.
A choir of souls, we rise and sing,
Transcendent steps, our hearts take wing.

Rising Tides of Hope

The ocean whispers, soft and low,
Its waves tell tales of dreams that flow.
With every tide, a promise made,
Of better days, a bright cascade.

In moonlit nights, the stars align,
Their light a beacon, pure, divine.
Each rise and fall, a gentle sigh,
Rising tides, together we try.

Through storms that shake and winds that wail,
We stand as one, we will not pale.
For in our hearts, the fire burns,
A flame of hope that always turns.

So let the waves crash at our feet,
With every challenge, we'll compete.
In rising tides, we find our fate,
A world reborn, we celebrate.

The Alchemy of Change

From ashes rise, the phoenix bold,
In every heart, a story told.
The alchemy of time and grace,
Transforms the pain, we find our place.

Through trials faced and lessons learned,
In every twist, a lantern burned.
With open minds, we dare to seek,
The golden thread in every streak.

As seasons shift from night to day,
The colors blend, they dance and sway.
In every drop, a chance to grow,
The alchemy of life, we sow.

So let us bound in joy and strife,
Embrace the magic of this life.
For in the change, we find our song,
The alchemy of hearts, lifelong.

A New Chapter Unfolds

Pages turning, crisp and bright,
Stories waiting for our light.
Each word a key, each line a door,
A new chapter, forevermore.

With hopeful hearts, we pen our dreams,
In ink of courage, flowing beams.
The past behind, the future near,
In every line, we shed our fear.

Through valleys dark and mountains steep,
The tales we weave, the seeds we reap.
With every breath, a fresh embrace,
A new chapter, our sacred space.

Together we write our destiny,
In harmony, we fly and see.
For in this life, our stories blend,
A new chapter, with love to mend.

Chasing Tomorrow's Dreams

In the hush of dawn, we soar,
With hopes that whisper evermore.
Each step we take, a path untold,
Chasing dreams that shimmer bold.

The sky paints hues of amber light,
As we dance through the fleeting night.
With every heartbeat, we believe,
In the wonders that we weave.

Though shadows linger, strife may come,
Our spirits rise like beating drums.
As we run toward the sun's embrace,
We craft our world, a sacred space.

Together we'll forge the stars above,
In the tapestry of dreams and love.
With courage bright, we'll find our way,
Chasing tomorrow, come what may.

Pilgrimage of the Heart

On paths where sunlight gently falls,
We seek the truth in nature's calls.
With every step, our burdens cease,
In valleys deep, we find our peace.

The heart, a compass, leads us through,
In every glance, the world feels new.
Each moment shared, a sacred thread,
In this pilgrimage, our souls are fed.

We wander far, through hills and streams,
In quiet whispers, we chase our dreams.
Embracing love along the way,
In life's great journey, we shall stay.

Together bound by hope's soft light,
In the darkest hours, shining bright.
With every heartbeat, we discover,
The sacred bond that joins each lover.

Strands of New Beginnings

In dawn's first light, the world awakes,
A canvas fresh, where beauty makes.
Each moment blooms like flowers rare,
Strands of new life fill the air.

With every tear, a lesson learned,
Through trials faced, our spirits burned.
The past is gone, and hope remains,
New beginnings burst from life's veins.

Like rivers flow to oceans wide,
We leave behind what once would hide.
Embrace the change, let courage ring,
In every heart, new joy can spring.

Together we weave the future's thread,
Through woven hopes, where fears have fled.
In unity, we rise anew,
Strands of life in vibrant hue.

Awakening Between the Stars

In the stillness of the night sky,
We find our dreams that dare to fly.
With every wish upon a star,
We awaken truths that shine from afar.

The universe whispers secrets grand,
In cosmic dance, we take our stand.
Caught between the vast unknown,
Our spirits soar as love has grown.

In midnight's grace, we grasp the light,
With hearts that pulse in shared delight.
The stars align in perfect sync,
Awakening magic, as we think.

With every heartbeat, we reclaim,
The spark of life, the cosmic flame.
Together, we rise, no fear, nor scars,
Awakening bold, between the stars.

Ripples of Change

In the calm of dawn's light,
Waves gently start to shift,
A whisper of hope spreads wide,
With each pulse, a new gift.

The waters, once so still,
Breathe life into the shore,
Each ripple speaks of will,
A chance to be much more.

Beneath the surface deep,
Life stirs with vibrant dreams,
Awake from tranquil sleep,
In currents, truth redeems.

Change flows like a stream,
Transforming every face,
A dance of light and gleam,
Embracing time and space.

The Compass of Rediscovery

Lost amidst the maze's twists,
We wander through the night,
Guided by the heart's insist,
Following the inner light.

Questions linger in the air,
With each step, truths unfurl,
Maps drawn from hope and care,
In this vast and swirling world.

Every turn reveals new ways,
Paths that lead to the unknown,
In the quiet, courage stays,
A compass of our own.

Forging bonds both old and new,
Finding strength in what we seek,
With each moment, courage grew,
As we embrace the unique.

Harmony in the Pause

In silence, there's a song,
A breath between each thought,
Moments linger, soft and long,
In stillness, peace is sought.

Time slows down, the heart aligns,
With whispers of the soul,
Finding rhythm in the signs,
As we start to feel whole.

The world turns with gentle grace,
In pauses, depth is found,
In the quiet, we embrace,
A harmony profound.

Let the stillness softly lead,
As we gather, we create,
In these pauses, hearts will feed,
On the love that we await.

Sentiments of a New Journey

With each step, new horizons call,
A canvas fresh and bright,
In every rise and subtle fall,
We chase the morning light.

Footprints mark the untold path,
Stories woven with care,
Embracing joy, facing wrath,
In the journey, we dare.

Memories blend like colors bright,
Painted with laughter and tears,
In the depth of day and night,
We conquer all our fears.

As the road unfolds its wings,
Adventure whispers loud,
With the joy each moment brings,
We walk our dreams unbowed.

Breath of a New Era

In the morning light we stand anew,
Dreams awaken under skies so blue.
Echoes of change in the gentle breeze,
Whispers of hope among the towering trees.

Casting away shadows of yesterday,
Embracing the dawn in a bold display.
Each heartbeat sings to a rhythm of grace,
As we step forward, we find our place.

With each breath, a promise unfolds,
The future listened, the past now told.
Ripples of courage begin to ignite,
Inspiring us all to shine so bright.

Together we gather, united in cheer,
The breath of a new era calls us near.
As we chase horizons painted in gold,
A tapestry woven, our stories told.

Awakening Each Dawn

Every sunrise brings a gift so rare,
A canvas stretched, free from despair.
Gentle hues of orange and pink,
Inch by inch, our spirits link.

With every chirp and soft morning sigh,
Nature's chorus bids the night goodbye.
Birds take flight in a dance so sweet,
Awakening dreams at our feet.

We rise with the sun, hearts open wide,
Wiping the slate of the night aside.
Each moment cherished, we seize the play,
Awakening each dawn, we find our way.

With laughter and love, we greet the light,
Fostering joy in the warmth of sight.
Together we wander, together we roam,
Awakening each dawn, we build our home.

The Voyage of Transformation

Set sail upon the vast unknown,
In the heart of change, we find our own.
Waves of wisdom crash and rise,
Guiding us toward clearer skies.

With every sunset, we shed our skin,
Emboldened by the courage within.
The tides may shift, the winds may wail,
But we are destined to thrive and sail.

Embrace the storms, for therein lies,
The seeds of growth, the chance to rise.
Navigating through fears, we chart our course,
Transforming pain into our source.

Together we voyage, hand in hand,
Building a future on shifting sand.
In the heart of the tempest, we find our song,
The voyage of transformation makes us strong.

Inner Landscapes Reclaimed

In the silence of the soul, we return,
To gardens lost, where memories churn.
With each breath, we plant a seed,
Nurturing the paths that we truly need.

Winding trails of past and present merge,
In vibrant colors, our spirits surge.
Through valleys deep, we rise and fall,
Listening closely to the inner call.

Mountains rise where fears once stood,
Transforming shadows into good.
In every corner, a story unfolds,
Inner landscapes reclaimed, a world that molds.

With open hearts, we seek to find,
The beauty hidden, the ties that bind.
In the tapestry of self, we weave and roam,
Reclaiming the landscapes that bring us home.

Vibrant Awakening

Morning blooms with golden hues,
Awakening dreams in endless views.
Birds sing sweet songs of the dawn,
Nature whispers, life reborn.

Soft breezes dance through waving trees,
Carrying scents of blossoms and bees.
In every corner, joy ignites,
A vibrant world in dazzling sights.

Sunlight kisses the glistening dew,
Painting earth in a radiant hue.
With each ray, a promise unfolds,
In vibrant strokes, our story told.

Hearts align with the sky so clear,
Embracing moments, drawing near.
In this dawning light, we rise,
A symphony of life that never dies.

Seeds of Self-Discovery

In the quiet of whispered dreams,
Lies a journey sewn at the seams.
Seeds of truth buried deep within,
Awakening tales where we begin.

Nurtured by the rains of time,
Growing strong, reaching for the climb.
Every struggle, every scar,
Guiding us to who we are.

The heart knows paths that eyes can't see,
Fertile ground for what we can be.
In the silence, a voice calls clear,
Discovering self, shedding fear.

Gentle sparks ignite the soul,
Through the darkness, we seek our goal.
Each step forward, a clearer view,
Seeds sprout forth, a life anew.

Awakening the Inner Light

Deep within, a flicker glows,
A quiet strength that gently grows.
In stillness, we begin to seek,
The inner voice, both strong and meek.

With each breath, we fan the flame,
Embracing all without the shame.
Resilience in the shadows shines,
Awakening truths, our spirit aligns.

Unseen forces guide the way,
Turning darkness into day.
In every heartbeat, truth revealed,
The inner light becomes our shield.

Rise and shine, let go of the night,
Embody hope, embrace the light.
In each moment, we take flight,
Awakening our inner light.

A Canvas Reimagined

Blank slate awaits, a brush in hand,
Dreams entwine, imaginings stand.
Colors blend with whispers of fate,
Creating worlds we contemplate.

Each stroke tells a story unwound,
In splashes of joy, our truths are found.
Lines dance freely, chaos appears,
A masterpiece crafted through hopes and fears.

Within the art, emotions flow,
Shapes and shades in ebb and glow.
A canvas alive, breathing its song,
Inviting all to come along.

From vibrant chaos, a vision gleams,
Transforming life into vivid dreams.
With each touch, our spirits rise,
A canvas reimagined beneath the skies.

Reimagined Strength

In quiet corners, courage grows,
Finding power in softer flows.
Each scar a story, a tale well spun,
In the heart, a battle has already won.

With every tear that paints the ground,
A deeper wisdom can be found.
Resilience blooms where shadows lay,
In the strength of night, we forge our day.

Hands that tremble, but never break,
Awakening dreams with every ache.
Trust in the journey, trust in the drive,
In the fleeting moments, we truly thrive.

Reimagined strength, a rising tide,
In the depths of struggle, we take pride.
Gathering fragments to build anew,
In the heart of the storm, we find what's true.

Shifting Sands of Self

Caught between memories and future's call,
In the shifting sands, we sometimes fall.
Each moment whispers of who we are,
Yet longing pulls us, like a distant star.

Waves that shape us, both gentle and fierce,
In each illusion, a truth we pierce.
The dance of identity, fluid and wide,
Embrace the change, let the current guide.

Layers of armor, slowly shed,
In the sun's warm light, we find our thread.
With every step on this winding shore,
The self keeps changing, forevermore.

Finding peace in the ebb and flow,
Letting go of what we think we know.
In the shifting sands, we learn to see,
The beauty in becoming, just let it be.

Flourish in the Light

Awake to dawn, a new day sings,
In the warmth of hope, the spirit springs.
Petals unfurling, colors ablaze,
In the gentle sun, we dance and gaze.

Roots that dig deep, tethered with care,
Nourished by dreams, thriving in air.
Embrace the glow, let shadows retreat,
In the light of love, we become complete.

Every heartbeat, a rhythm divine,
Echoes of joy, in every line.
Breathe in the beauty, let worries wane,
In the tapestry of life, we find our gain.

Flourish and bloom, let spirits take flight,
In gardens of wonder, we claim our right.
With laughter and kindness, our burdens grow light,
We find our way home, in the warmest light.

The Odyssey of Healing

A journey begins where the heart feels lost,
Navigating waters, no matter the cost.
With every ripple, a lesson appears,
Casting aside the weight of our fears.

Each step a whisper, a voice of the past,
In the fabric of time, our shadows are cast.
Yet beneath the storm, seeds start to sprout,
In the quiet, we hear what life's about.

Sailing through tempests, we learn to forgive,
Finding the strength in the will to live.
The horizon beckons, a promise of light,
In the odyssey of healing, we reclaim our might.

Though scars may linger, they tell our tale,
Each heart's journey, a mighty sail.
Together we rise, through sorrow and grace,
In the dance of healing, we find our place.

The Art of Reinvention

In shadows cast by doubt's cruel hand,
A spark emerges, making a stand.
With every step, the past unwinds,
A canvas fresh, where hope binds.

Colors blend in a dance so bright,
We sketch new dreams beneath the night.
The whispers of change, a guiding sound,
In the heart's embrace, new paths are found.

Each layer peeled reveals the core,
An open mind invites much more.
From ashes rise the flames anew,
For in our hearts, we hold what's true.

So let the tides of fate reshape,
A new design, a daring cape.
In the art of life, embrace the flow,
In every end, a chance to grow.

Nourishing the Soul

In silence deep, the spirit breathes,
A gentle balm, the heart receives.
With every note of nature's song,
A sacred space, where we belong.

The warmth of sun, the moon's soft glow,
In rituals of love, we come to know.
To nourish dreams, to heal the scars,
In starlit nights, we find our stars.

Through laughter shared and tears released,
We feast on moments, joy increased.
With open arms, the world we greet,
In kindness sown, our souls entreat.

So take a breath, let stillness reign,
For in this calm, we break each chain.
To feed the spirit, let love take flight,
In the quiet hours, we find our light.

Flight toward the Horizon

With wings unfurled, the journey starts,
A leap of faith, igniting hearts.
Through clouds that dance in bright delight,
We chase the dawn, embrace the light.

The whispering winds, they call us near,
In every heartbeat, we persevere.
Over valleys deep and mountains high,
We soar as one, our spirits fly.

Beyond the borders of what we know,
New landscapes beckon, hope will grow.
With open skies and dreams in sight,
We chase the horizon, feel the flight.

Together we weave our tales untold,
In every clash, in moments bold.
For as we rise, the world unfolds,
In unity, our journey molds.

Echoes of the Heart

In secret chambers, memories dwell,
Whispers of love that time can't quell.
A heartbeat's rhythm, soft and clear,
In every echo, I hold you near.

From distant past, the voices call,
In laughter shared, in shadows small.
A tapestry woven with every thread,
In every heartbeat, the stories spread.

Through joy and sorrow, the music flows,
In every pause, affection shows.
The echoes linger, timeless yet,
In the heart's embrace, we don't forget.

So let the echoes softly chime,
In every moment, the threads of time.
For love's refrain, a song so sweet,
In echoes of the heart, we meet.

Seeds of Resilience

In cracks of stone, they find a way,
Tiny seeds that dream and sway.
Through storms and trials, they will grow,
With every struggle, they'll bestow.

Roots dig deep in soil's embrace,
Nurtured by time, they find their place.
A whisper soft, a silent shout,
In each small seed, strength is sprout.

Against the wind, they stand so tall,
Each setback faced, they never fall.
With open hearts, they greet the sun,
In unity, their race is run.

Together strong, they weave their tale,
Through every winter, they won't pale.
For life's a journey, bold and bright,
In seeds of hope, we find our light.

The Dance of Renewal

In springtime's bloom, the world awakens,
With vibrant hues, new life is taken.
A gentle breeze, a fragrant sigh,
In nature's arms, our spirits fly.

Each cycle spins, a tale retold,
Of warmth and light, a heart of gold.
With every leaf that starts to sway,
The dance of life begins to play.

As seasons turn, the colors change,
In every heart, the rhythms range.
From earth to sky, we sway and twirl,
In unity, a precious whirl.

And through it all, we learn to see,
The beauty found in harmony.
As blossoms open, let love flow,
In every step, the dance we know.

From Shadows to Light

In quiet corners, shadows creep,
Yet in their depths, the secrets sleep.
A flicker dim, a spark untamed,\nIn darkness, strength is
often claimed.

The night will fade, the dawn will rise,
With golden hues that fill the skies.
From gloom to glow, the journey's made,
In every heart, hope won't evade.

Each whispered thought becomes a flame,
Illuminating what's been lame.
From shadows cast, we find our way,
With courage bold, we dare to stay.

So let us dance, let spirits soar,
From shadows deep, we'll rise and roar.
For in the light, our dreams take flight,
Transforming fear to purest light.

Threads of Vitality

With every breath, we weave a strand,
Of joy and pain, both hand in hand.
In tapestry of life we find,
The threads that bind, our hearts aligned.

As seasons shift, the colors blend,
Each moment lived, a message penned.
In laughter's song and sorrow's tear,
We find the strength to persevere.

With tender care, we tie the knots,
Embracing all, forgetting not.
For every thread, a story tells,
Of resilience found in life's swells.

In every heart, a vibrant hue,
The tapestry grows, both old and new.
Together, strong, we intertwine,
In threads of life, our spirits shine.

Aspiration's Flame

In the heart, a fire glows,
Dreams take wing, as courage grows.
With every step, we rise anew,
The light within will guide us through.

Chasing shadows, crossing fears,
Voices whisper, drawing near.
Hope ignites like stars at night,
A beacon's glow, our guiding light.

Through the storm, we stand tall,
Embracing life, we heed the call.
With passion's spark, we'll persevere,
In every heart, the flame is clear.

And when we stumble, when we fall,
We'll find the strength, we'll stand up tall.
For in our souls, the fire burns bright,
Aspiration's flame is our birthright.

Serenade of Change

Whispers of the winds of time,
Nature sings in silent rhyme.
Leaves will dance and rivers flow,
Embracing all that we don't know.

Breaking dawn with hues so bright,
Every moment feels so right.
Life's a melody, sweet and strange,
The world awakens, sings of change.

From shadows deep, new paths will rise,
In every heart, a dream that flies.
The harmony of life unfolds,
Every story yet untold.

Listen close, the stars will speak,
With every pulse, future peaks.
Together, we will brave the range,
In unity, we learn to change.

Epicenter of Evolution

In the center, life begins,
A dance of cells, where hope prespins.
Progress woven through each day,
In whispers small, we find our way.

From the roots, growth spirals wide,
Ancient tales in us abide.
Rising high, like mountains tall,
In the journey, we discover all.

Echoes of the past resound,
In every heartbeat, truth is found.
Embrace the change, the world spins fast,
In evolution, shadows cast.

From the depths to the skies above,
In every heartbeat, feel the love.
Together, we will reshape fate,
In this epicenter, we create.

Harmonies of New Life

Softly blooms the day's first light,
Nature whispers, pure delight.
Every seed with dreams to strive,
In vast gardens, all will thrive.

Cycles turn, and seasons play,
In their dance, we find our way.
From quiet nights to mornings bright,
Harmonies of life ignite.

With every heartbeat, life unfolds,
In stories shared and dreams retold.
Together in this vibrant sphere,
New lives form, our purpose clear.

Embrace the change, the joy, the pain,
In every lesson, wisdom gained.
With open hearts, we rise and dive,
In these harmonies, we come alive.

From Shadows to Radiance

In the quiet dusk we find,
A flicker lost in time.
Whispers calling, fears unwind,
From shadows, hope will climb.

With every dawn, a chance to rise,
Beneath the golden gleam.
Our dreams aloft, like birds that fly,
A tapestry of beam.

The night retreats, its grip now light,
As colors start to blend.
Emerging from the cover tight,
We greet the day, our friend.

From darkness into vibrant glow,
We walk the path anew.
In every heart, a brighter flow,
For shadows serve their due.

The Dance of Restoration

In nature's arms, we sway and twirl,
The earth's embrace, a gentle curl.
Through storms and calm, we sing of grace,
Each heartbeat finds its rightful place.

With every step, the world revives,
Lost dreams awaken, hope survives.
The silent prayers of ancient trees,
In rustling leaves, we feel the breeze.

With colors bright, the canvas forms,
In unity, we brave the storms.
Restoration's song, a melody,
That wraps the heart in harmony.

Together we dance, hand in hand,
In sacred circles, we make our stand.
For in the joy of life's ballet,
We find our path, come what may.

Embracing the Unknown

Underneath the vast expanse,
A world awaits, unseen by chance.
With open hearts, we take the leap,
Into the depths where secrets sleep.

The stars above, a guiding light,
In shadows cast, we see the bright.
Each step unwinds a thread of fate,
To relish change, we celebrate.

In whispered winds, new tales unfold,
The stories waiting to be told.
As we embrace what lies ahead,
A journey blooms, our hearts are fed.

With courage found in every breath,
We dance with life, defying death.
In unknown paths, our spirits soar,
For every door leads to much more.

Painted by the Seasons

Spring blossoms bright, life starts anew,
With vibrant hues in morning dew.
The air is sweet, as petals fall,
In painted strokes, we hear the call.

Summer's warmth in golden rays,
The laughter shared on sun-kissed days.
In fields we run, with dreams in tow,
A canvas wide, where love can grow.

Autumn whispers in shades of gold,
As leaves let go, their stories told.
The crisp air brings a tranquil peace,
A time for change, where all can cease.

Winter's breath, a quiet grace,
In softened hush, our souls embrace.
Through cycles vast, life carries on,
Each season sings, a timeless song.

Renewed Reflections

In quiet pools the thoughts reside,
With whispers soft, they gently glide.
Each wave reveals a hidden truth,
Reflecting dreams of forgotten youth.

The sun illuminates the past,
Moments fleeting, shadows cast.
With every ripple, change begins,
A dance of joy that never ends.

New visions spark with every glance,
A chance to shine, a bold advance.
Embrace the now, let go the fears,
In renewed light, wash away the tears.

So let the waters guide the way,
Transform the night into the day.
In renewed reflections, soar above,
Unveil the life you truly love.

The Garden Within

In the garden where we sow,
Seeds of hope begin to grow.
Petals soft, in colors bright,
Blooming gently, pure delight.

Roots run deep through fears and doubt,
Nurtured whispers, dreams shout out.
Every flower tells a tale,
Of love's strength, it will prevail.

Breezes carry scents so sweet,
Nature's heart gives life a beat.
In this space, we find our peace,
The garden thrives, our joy's increase.

So pause and breathe, let silence reign,
In your garden, soothe the pain.
Cultivate the love you find,
In the garden deep inside.

Metamorphosis of Mind and Body

In twilight's glow, the change begins,
A whisper stirs, the soul spins.
From shadows dark to radiant light,
Awakening in sacred flight.

The body learns to shed the old,
Fragmented stories, secrets told.
With every breath, a rebirth calls,
As past illusions gently fall.

The mind expands, horizons spread,
In unison, where once was dread.
Transformation blooms with every day,
A vivid dance that leads the way.

So honor this, your own showcase,
In metamorphosis, find your grace.
Embrace the change, with open arms,
For life is rich with endless charms.

Rising from the Ashes

Beneath the rubble, light awaits,
A flicker bright that resonates.
From fiery trials, we arise,
Resilient hearts, the flames disguise.

With every ember, strength ignites,
Turning darkness into sights.
From cinders gray to vibrant hue,
Renewal sings in every hue.

The past may haunt, but hope prevails,
A phoenix rises, strong, it sails.
With wings outstretched, it graces skies,
A symbol of the boldest rise.

So when despair begins to creep,
Recall the ashes hold the deep.
In rising up, we find our home,
In every heart, we learn to roam.

The Symphony of Growth

In the garden of dreams, we sow,
Seeds of hope begin to grow.
With the sunlight, shadows fade,
New beginnings gently made.

Roots entwine beneath the earth,
Whispers tell of hidden worth.
Each petal, a story unfolds,
In colors bright, the future holds.

Nature's symphony plays on high,
Notes of laughter fill the sky.
Every breeze a sweet caress,
In this dance, we find our rest.

With each cycle that we embrace,
Life reveals its tender grace.
Through the trials we endure,
The symphony sings, strong and pure.

Breathing New Life

In quiet moments, hear the call,
Within the silence, life stands tall.
Every heartbeat is a song,
A reminder we all belong.

As dawn breaks with colors bright,
Hope awakens with the light.
A fresh start, like morning dew,
Breathing life into the new.

With every step upon this ground,
Miracles in the mundane found.
Life's rhythms, soft and sweet,
Make our journeys feel complete.

In the embrace of earth and sky,
We find solace, learn to fly.
Breathing deep, we soar above,
Unfolding each moment with love.

Wings of Resilience

In stormy skies, we find our way,
Through waves of doubt, we learn to sway.
Each struggle is a feathered part,
Crafting strength within the heart.

Like the phoenix, rise anew,
Burning bright in vibrant hue.
With every challenge, we take flight,
Harnessing the power of light.

Bound by courage, we embrace,
Every trial, a healing grace.
Through the darkness, we shall see,
Wings of resilience set us free.

Together we will forge ahead,
On paths where only few have tread.
With the wind beneath our wings,
We'll face whatever courage brings.

Echoes of a New Dawn

When night retreats and shadows flee,
The world awakens, wild and free.
Awash in colors, bold and bright,
Echoes arise to greet the light.

With every sunrise, dreams ignite,
Whispers of hope take graceful flight.
In the silence, we hear the call,
Embracing vision, one and all.

The past is but a distant song,
In the new day, we grow strong.
Together, let our spirits blend,
As echoes of the dawn transcend.

With open hearts, we face the morn,
In laughter and love, we are reborn.
In each moment, let's create,
An echo of love that won't abate.

Navigating the Current

In waters deep, we chart our course,
Against the tide, we feel its force.
With every wave, we learn to steer,
Embracing change, we cast our fear.

The currents pull, they twist and turn,
Through tempests fierce, we ebb and learn.
In stillness found, we seek the light,
Guiding us safely through the night.

A compass set by stars above,
Our hearts are true, we steer with love.
Each ripple tells a story bold,
In flowing waters, dreams unfold.

Together we sail, hand in hand,
Through uncharted seas, we make our stand.
Navigating life's endless stream,
With courage found, we chase our dream.

Rebirth in Full Color

From ashes rise, a phoenix bright,
New wings unfurling, catching light.
In vibrant hues, we find our voice,
Nature's palette, we rejoice.

The winter's chill melts into spring,
With blossoms fresh, the birds will sing.
Each petal kissed by morning dew,
A canvas rich with every hue.

In every shade, a tale begins,
Of heartbeats, losses, and quiet wins.
We paint our lives with strokes so bold,
In artful strokes, our truths unfold.

With every dawn, new visions gleam,
Rebirth awakens, life's sweet theme.
In colors bright, we rise anew,
Embracing all that is true to you.

Casting Off Old Skins

In shadows cast, we shed the past,
The grip of time, it cannot last.
With every layer, we drift apart,
Releasing chains that bound the heart.

The skin of doubt, we peel away,
Emerging strong with light of day.
In whispers soft, the truth we find,
A chance to bloom, to free the mind.

Each step we take, a breath anew,
Embracing growth, the quest to do.
With courage fierce, we forge ahead,
In shedding skins, we're truly led.

The past behind, a lesson learned,
In every scar, a page is turned.
With every change, we find the glow,
In casting off, our spirits flow.

The Art of Becoming

In every moment, we shape our fate,
Through twists and turns, we navigate.
An artist's touch, the canvas bare,
With dreams and hopes, we sculpt the air.

As seasons shift, we redefine,
A journey rich, with paths entwined.
Each choice we make, a brushstroke bright,
In the palette of our own delight.

With every tear, a lesson learned,
In every smile, the fire burned.
We weave our stories, thread by thread,
The art of becoming, love widespread.

In the tapestry of life, we find,
Reflections deep within the mind.
With open hearts, we craft and mold,
The art we share, a tale retold.

Drenched in New Beginnings

Morning dew on tender grass,
Whispers of hope as shadows pass.
Dreams awake from endless night,
Colors bloom in warm sunlight.

The world unfolds like a fresh page,
Every heart begins to wage.
A journey starts with each new breath,
Dancing towards the edge of death.

Sculpting Tomorrow's Vision

Chiseling dreams from solid stone,
Crafting futures we call our own.
With every strike, a shape appears,
Washing away our deepest fears.

Molding clay with gentle hands,
Visions rise from shifting sands.
The artist's heart, a beacon bright,
Guides us through the velvet night.

The Tapestry of Growth

Threads of life, both weak and strong,
Woven tales where we belong.
Each stitch a lesson, every tear,
Patterns form with utmost care.

In colors bold, through shades of gray,
Unexpected joys on display.
Seasons change to weave anew,
Unraveling the heart's true hue.

Resilient Roots

Deep in earth, where dreams abide,
Roots stretch wide, with strength and pride.
Through storms and trials that they face,
Holding fast, they find their place.

Nurtured by the sun and rain,
Bearing fruit through joy and pain.
In every setback, they stand tall,
Resilient spirits, never fall.

A Journey to Wholeness

In the silence, I find my heart's call,
Steps to healing, I will not fall.
With each breath, I gather my light,
Journeying inward, ready to fight.

In the shadows, my fears reside,
Yet with courage, I will abide.
Threads of hope weave through my soul,
In acceptance, I start to feel whole.

As I wander through valleys of doubt,
With every stumble, I learn about.
Pieces of me, scattered like stars,
Together I'll rise, no more scars.

The path ahead, both rugged and clear,
With each step forward, I conquer fear.
Embracing the journey, I find my way,
A tapestry of light, come what may.

Shaping the Future

Visions awaken with the dawn's glow,
Seeds of change in the winds that blow.
Hand in hand, we forge anew,
Crafting a world, me and you.

In every heart lies a dream that grows,
Cultivating hope where the river flows.
United we stand, as voices will cheer,
For together we'll break through every fear.

Every action, a ripple that spreads,
Nurturing roots where ambition treads.
Tomorrow awaits, we hold the key,
Shaping the future, setting it free.

With courage unyielding, we brave the night,
In the face of darkness, we are the light.
So let us rise and chart the course,
For the future is ours, fueled by our force.

Unfolding Inner Strength

Deep within, a fire ignites,
In the stillness, I embrace the heights.
Every challenge, a chance to grow,
Unfolding the power that I may not know.

In moments of struggle, I find my voice,
Courage blooms, a conscious choice.
With open hands, I face my fears,
Through trials and triumphs, I shed my tears.

The whispers of doubt, I cast aside,
Embracing the strength that's deep inside.
I rise like the phoenix, bold and free,
Unfolding the truth of who I can be.

Through every storm, I'm anchored strong,
In the dance of life, I find my song.
With resilience, I journey ahead,
Unfolding inner strength, I am led.

Radiance of the New Path

A new beginning, a dawn so bright,
Guided by stars in the velvet night.
With every step, a promise unfolds,
Radiance shines in the heart, so bold.

Embracing change, like the tide's flow,
Casting aside what I used to know.
In the whispers of nature, I find my way,
The light of the path calls me to stay.

Wounds that once marked the journey I tread,
Transform into lessons, a life well-led.
With courage as compass, I'm never lost,
For in every heartbeat, I count the cost.

With eyes wide open, I greet the dawn,
In the radiance of growth, I feel reborn.
With hope in my heart, I venture forth,
To embrace the new path, the true inner worth.

Climbing Higher

Step by step, we rise anew,
Reaching heights, breaking through.
Mountains call, their peaks so grand,
With every hold, we take a stand.

The skies above, a canvas wide,
With dreams of flight, we will abide.
The summit gleams, a beacon bright,
Guiding us toward the light.

In every struggle, strength is found,
With every breath, our hearts resound.
Together we ascend the slope,
In this ascent, we cling to hope.

When clouds may gather, doubts may loom,
We rise above, dispelling gloom.
With each new step, we claim our fate,
Climbing higher, we celebrate.

Embracing Change

In the winds of change we flow,
Like rivers twist, we learn to grow.
Seasons shift, and so must we,
In every ending, a chance to see.

Leaves may fall, yet roots stay strong,
In the dance of life, we belong.
Every turn brings lessons dear,
With open hearts, we persevere.

The unknown path, we bravely tread,
With courage bold, we move ahead.
Finding beauty in new sights,
Embracing change, igniting lights.

In the cycles, we find our grace,
Letting go, we'll find our place.
For through the storms, we'll rise again,
Embracing change, our greatest gain.

The Alchemy of Self

In the furnace of our soul,
We forge the parts that make us whole.
From base to gold, with time we learn,
To embrace the fire, let it burn.

Every trial becomes our muse,
Transforming pain, we choose to fuse.
From ashes rise a brand new start,
The alchemy of the human heart.

With every scar, a tale is spun,
The past a guide, yet we move on.
In shadows cast, the light will shine,
The magic lives within our mind.

So let us blend the old with new,
With faith and courage, we break through.
In every moment, choose to believe,
The alchemy of self, we weave.

Roots of Rebirth

Deep in the earth, our roots align,
Connected to the grand design.
From seed to tree, we grow and bend,
In every season, life transcends.

Through winter's chill and summer's sun,
The cycle turns, we're all but one.
In every fall, a chance awaits,
For rebirth blooms at heaven's gates.

With branches wide, we touch the sky,
In every whisper, dreams will fly.
Past's embrace, a strength we find,
The roots of rebirth, intertwined.

So let us nurture what we sow,
In faith and love, our spirits grow.
In every heartbeat, life will sing,
Roots of rebirth, new hope they bring.

An Odyssey to Self

In shadows deep, I search and find,
The pieces lost, the ties that bind.
With every step, I shed the old,
A story new, waiting to unfold.

The map is drawn on heart and soul,
A winding path towards the whole.
With courage fierce, I face my fear,
An odyssey, the end is near.

Each lesson learned, a guiding star,
In tranquil moments, I've come so far.
The mirror reflects the truth I see,
Embracing all that's meant to be.

Unraveling threads of doubt and pain,
In the silence, I break the chain.
The journey starts where I reside,
An odyssey to self inside.

The Garden Within

In the silence of the heart, I sow,
Seeds of kindness, watch them grow.
Petals bloom in colors bright,
A sanctuary, pure delight.

With whispers soft, the breezes play,
Guiding dreams that drift away.
Sunlight kisses every leaf,
In this garden, there's belief.

Roots entwined in earth so dear,
Holding close all I hold near.
Through storms that come, I stand my ground,
In this garden, peace is found.

Each flower tells a tale untold,
Of moments cherished, young and old.
In my garden, spirits soar,
A place of love, forevermore.

Constellations of Change

In the tapestry of night, I see,
Stars that whisper far and free.
Each twinkle speaks of moments lost,
A journey taken, no matter the cost.

From darkness blooms a light so bright,
Shadows dance in the pale moonlight.
New beginnings, a cosmic chance,
In every star, a hidden glance.

Comets blaze their trails of night,
Casting dreams in their fleeting flight.
With every flicker, echoes say,
That change is coming, come what may.

Galaxies spin in endless grace,
Reminding us of time and space.
Constellations guide the heart,
In the universe, we play our part.

Life's Rebirth

In the dawn's embrace, I rise anew,
With hope that glimmers, shining through.
A canvas fresh, unmarred by time,
Each heartbeat sings a vibrant rhyme.

Through trials faced, I learned to soar,
With every scar, I've grown much more.
The past will fade, like morning mist,
In life's rebirth, I find my bliss.

Butterflies break from their cocoon,
Transforming dreams beneath the moon.
With open arms, I greet the day,
In life's rebirth, I find my way.

Each season brings a chance to grow,
In rhythms of nature, life's sweet flow.
With every turn, I embrace the light,
Life's rebirth, a wondrous sight.